trotman

REAL LIFE ISSUES:
MONEY

Dee Pilgrim

Real Life Issues: Money
This first edition published in 2004 by Trotman and Company Ltd
2 The Green, Richmond, Surrey TW9 1PL

© Trotman and Company Limited 2004

Editorial and Publishing Team
Author Dee Pilgrim
Editorial Mina Patria, Editorial Director; Rachel Lockhart, Commissioning Editor;
Anya Wilson, Managing Editor; Bianca Knights, Assistant Editor
Production Ken Ruskin, Head of Pre-press and Production;
James Rudge, Production Artworker
Sales and Marketing Deborah Jones, Head of Sales and Marketing
Advertising Tom Lee, Commercial Director
Managing Director Toby Trotman

Designed by XAB

British Library Cataloguing in Publication Data
A catalogue record for this book is available from the British Library

ISBN 0 85660 988 9

Typeset by Tradespools Publishing Solutions
Printed and bound in Great Britain by
Cromwell Press, Trowbridge, Wiltshire

CONTENTS:

'... you can become master or mistress of your financial fortune, rather than letting it rule you.'

REAL LIFE ISSUES:
Money

ABOUT THE AUTHOR

Dee Pilgrim completed the pre-entry, periodical journalism course at the London College of Printing before working on a variety of music and women's titles. As a freelancer and full-time member of staff, she has written numerous articles and interviews for *Company*, *Cosmopolitan, New Woman, Woman's Journal* and *Weight Watchers* magazines. For many years she covered new output by singer/songwriters for *Top* magazine, which was distributed via Tower record stores, and during this period interviewed the likes of Tori Amos, Tom Robinson and Joan Armatrading. As a freelancer for Independent Magazines, she concentrated on celebrity interviews and film, theatre and restaurant reviews for such titles as *Ms London, Girl About Town, LAM* and *Nine To Five* magazines and, in her capacity as a critic, she has appeared on both radio and television. She is currently the film reviewer for *Now* Magazine. When not attending film screenings, she is active within the Critics' Circle and is on the committee for their annual film awards' event. Dee is a published songwriter and is currently engaged in writing the narrative to an as yet unpublished trilogy of children's illustrated books.

REAL LIFE ISSUES:
Money

ACKNOWLEDGEMENTS

I could not have undertaken the writing of this book without the help of a great many people. Mr Omar Mohammed, the Media Relations Manager for the Royal Bank of Scotland, was instrumental in making me aware of their Face 2 Face with Finance initiative, now being taught in many schools throughout the UK (see Resources). Josie Clapham, the Head of Students and Graduate Banking at HSBC, provided many quotes on the spending power and attitudes of young people towards money. Thank you to Jenny Catlin, Consumer Analyst with Mintel Market Research Group, for offering in-depth insights into its 'Pocket Money – Food and Drink' report (2004), and to the Sutton Trust for details of its 'School Omnibus' report (2004), carried out by Mori. Finally, a huge big thank you to all the young people who talked so openly and honestly about what money means to them, including the pupils of The Gregg School in Hampshire, Isabel Rose, Alice-Lara Waterman and Paul Welsh.

INTRODUCTION
Taking control of your money

Money: none of us can live without it but, boy, living with it can be hard! We worry that if we go to university, we won't be able to pay back our student loan; that when we leave school we won't get a job that pays us enough to live on; that we won't be able to save enough for the deposit on a flat; that we're not saving at all; that we're spending too much; that as fast as it comes in, it runs straight back out again; and that if that rainy day does actually arrive, there won't be enough in the coffers to deal with it. Money: it's enough to give you nightmares! But it doesn't have to be that way. By learning as much as you can about money and having a positive attitude, you can become master or mistress of your financial future, rather than letting it rule you.

SPENDING: WHAT ARE THE FACTS?

Young people today have more disposable income than they have ever had before. Apparently, Britain's 16-year-olds are worth a record £2.1 billion (source: The Royal Bank of Scotland) and, like almost everybody else on the planet, they like to spend it. They spend it on going out, on branded goods such as clothing, footwear, mobiles and gadgets, and on entertainment such as CDs, computer games and DVDs.

However, having disposable income doesn't mean young people are knowledgeable about money matters, nor does it stop them from worrying about it. Over 50 per cent of GCSE pupils admit they lack a fundamental knowledge about financial matters. In a recent report by the Royal Bank of Scotland, 49 per cent of the young people questioned said they did not feel confident about writing out a cheque, while 76 per cent admitted they had no idea what a direct debit was.

DEBT: WHAT ARE THE FACTS?

Ignorance about money matters isn't their only concern: they also worry about getting into debt. Unbelievably, Britain's personal debt has just passed the £1 trillion mark for the first time. That's the equivalent of £17,000 of debt for every man, woman and child in the UK. In a recent study for the Sutton Trust, 20 per cent of the young people questioned said fear of debt would stop them from going on to university, with the figure rising to 30 per cent for young people whose parents were out of work. If money worries can affect a life decision as important as taking up a place at university, then it's an issue that must really be addressed and dealt with. It pays (in all senses of the word) to have a good understanding of how money works, to have a good emotional response to money, and to be in control of your finances.

Josie Clapham, the head of Students and Graduate Banking for HSBC, knows only too well the importance of educating young people in financial matters:

'It's amazing that so many young people do want to have the feeling of (financial) independence at such an early age and be in control of their money, and understand that paying in is a good thing and stands them in good stead for future years. It's very important from an early age to understand the benefits of saving. As an individual it gives you a sense of freedom and achievement. We live in a world where (getting into) debt is made so easy that we responsible lenders feel it is in our interests to educate our up-and-coming adult customers about finances and debt.'

However, Josie Clapham also acknowledges that it is almost inevitable that most people (around 95 per cent) who go on to higher education will come out of it with some level of debt:

'From research we know that students realise they probably will end up in debt, but it is how they manage that debt that is important. I see more and more of them working during the holidays because they know they need to help with fees. Teenagers these days are much more aware of what lies ahead and many more are now supplementing their income. It's about, "I know I will get into debt because I have a lot to pay for, so how do I mitigate that, and what support systems are there to help me?"'

If you worry about money and all it entails, from writing a cheque to balancing your books, then you are in good company. Like anything else in life, starting something new is always slightly scary, so if you've never dealt with your own money before, it is perfectly natural to feel nervous about doing so. Josie acknowledges that walking into a bank can be the most daunting of endeavours, but believes that:

'We in the banking industry are waking up in terms of understanding young people today, and so are gearing services to them. Banks definitely do have more of an open-door policy these days, so people do engage with us. Communication, both inbound and outbound, is much more proactive with our young customers. What everybody hopes for is that students and young people will come out of their education with a good, healthy attitude towards money.'

WHAT IS THIS BOOK ABOUT?

This is what this book is here for. If you've picked it up, it probably means in the first place that you want to find out more about money, about how it works and how you can learn to manage it efficiently. Within these pages you will find practical advice on everything from opening a bank account to choosing the right bank for you. Equally importantly, the book will help you assess whether your emotional response to money is a healthy one and if not, show you ways of modifying that response. Having good money sense and the right attitude will give you a head start in the money stakes. It will help ensure you know how to deal with debt if you go to university, and give you the knowledge that will help you to budget with your weekly allowance and to save for your first property. It will also help you keep good financial records (an absolute bonus if you want to go to the bank for a startup loan to launch your own company). The aim is to put you in control of your financial situation so you can get on with the things that really matter – like spending that lovely cash you were sensible enough to save in the first place.

'I believe in an ideal world there would be no money and everything would be shared. Nevertheless, money is necessary in everyday life.'

James Williams, 14

CHAPTER ONE:

HOW DO YOU FEEL ABOUT MONEY?
Do you control it or does it control you?

As you will have seen from the introduction to this book, your attitude towards money and personal finances can have a very real effect on your future prospects and life choices. That is why it is important to make sure your relationship with money is a healthy and confident one. You may not be aware of it, but your own emotional response to money will be affected by many things, not least your family's financial situation. For example, if money has always been short in your household and you or your parents have had to really save hard to buy things such as new trainers or jeans, you will view money in a different way from someone whose family has a high disposable income and can buy these items easily, without affecting the family budget.

Other things that affect the way you view money include your susceptibility to advertising and peer pressure, and whether you are a naturally optimistic person, or timid and fearful of what the future might hold. The financial world around us is changing rapidly: in an era where you can secure a loan from the high street supermarket and transact your financial business over the Internet, it pays for you to be in control of your money and not have it control you.

'Money makes me feel happy, but I'd rather be happy with a little money than depressed with loads of money.'

Jenny Willbourn, 14

'Money means power and fun and excitement and hard work. Having money makes me feel I can do anything.'

Paul Welsh, 13

The following five questions are aimed at giving you a better idea of the way you look at money issues. There are no wrong or right answers, so be totally honest with yourself.

ARE YOU IN CONTROL OF YOUR MONEY?

1 *Are you fully aware of your own financial situation?*

2 *Do you know how much you spend a week and what you spend it on?*

3 *Do you save regularly, or at all?*

4 *Do you keep a record of what you earn (pocket money/Saturday job) and what you spend, and check it against your bank statements (if you have a bank account)?*

5 *Do you understand the charges for your mobile phone (if you have one) and the way the tariff works?*

If most of your answers were 'yes', then you are probably well on the way to being in control of your money. However, if you answered 'no' to one or all of the above, it could be you have never seriously thought about money before. If this is the case, then now is a really good time to start. Getting into good financial habits early in life could save you from all sorts of nasty messes later on.

'Money means pretty much everything. Money means a nice house, nice car, nice clothes and nice holiday. I mean, there isn't much you can do without money.'

Alice-Lara Waterman, 16

WHAT IS YOUR EMOTIONAL RESPONSE TO MONEY?

The following quiz will explore your emotional response to money more fully. Just tick the answer you think is closest to the way you feel or would react. Once again, there are no wrong or right answers, so be as honest with yourself as you can.

1 One of your friends has just bought the new Sony HiMD Player that can store up to 45 CDs on one 1Gb MiniDisc. Do you:

a Congratulate them on the purchase but, as you know it is out of your price range, not even think about having one yourself?

b Think it's really cool and work out how much you will need to save each week in order to buy one?

c Go so green with envy that you don't think about the cost, but raid your piggy bank/savings and buy one immediately?

2 You are thinking of going on to university after leaving school. The thought of taking out a student loan:

a Fills you with dread – how will you ever pay it back?

b Seems like a good idea if it is going to finance the education you need to get a better job?

c The thought never enters your head: it's much too far in the future to even consider?

3 Your bank sends you monthly statements for your current and savings accounts. Do you:

a Put them in a drawer to be opened later?

b Open them immediately to see if there are any discrepancies between the statements and your own records?

c Not bother to open them and put them straight in the bin?

4 A distant relative has died and left you a large sum of money. Do you:

a Put it all into a high interest savings account – well, you never know what tomorrow might bring?

b Invest some of it, but keep a sum back to pay for something you really need or want (driving lessons/a new computer game)?

c Spend it all – it's yours isn't it?

5 How does spending money make you feel?

a Anxious – you never know where the next pound is going to come from?

b OK – you spend within your means and stay in control?

c Happy – who cares about tomorrow: today is to be enjoyed?

6 You want to upgrade your mobile phone, what do you do next?

a Upgrading may mean incurring higher costs, so you decide to stick with the one you've got?

b Go and do some research at your local mobile phone store to see which network can give you the best deal – making sure you check the small print?

c Choose the latest generation tri-band phone with digital camera and zoom? It's expensive but you think you're worth it.

7 You've managed to spend all your monthly budget on one blow-out weekend. The only problem is your best friend's birthday is coming up and they are planning a trip to the cinema and a meal afterwards. Do you:

a Decide to cry off – you know they'll be disappointed but you are too ashamed to tell them you have no money?

b Explain the situation to your mum or dad and see if they can give you an advance on your allowance to tide you over?

c Borrow the money from another friend – you'll pay them back when you can?

8 The best way for you to ensure a secure financial future is:

a Spend as little as possible, but worry you won't ever be financially secure?

b Budget well, work hard and make sure you save regularly?

c Win the lottery or *Who Wants To Be A Millionaire?*

9 Having money makes you feel:

a Secure and safe, but also worried it may disappear?

b In control of your life?

c More attractive and popular as a person?

10 To you, money is:

a A necessary evil and something to be feared?

b A tool to be used wisely and responsibly?

c To be spent?

How to score the quiz

Count up how many of your answers are A, B, or C. You may have a mix of all three, but if you find you have many more of one than the others, this can tell you an awful lot about your emotional response to money.

MOSTLY As

You feel anxious about money and that anxiety is affecting what you do with your life. It could be that your family background is one where money has been scarce or where money problems have caused stress, leading you to worry about every penny. Even when money is around, you still worry that it might disappear – and then you worry about what you are going to do if it does! You need to get a better and more positive perspective on financial matters, then you won't feel so anxious. If you know yourself to be in control of your finances and able to deal with money efficiently, your worries will disappear. Money is a means to getting the most out of life, but it should not control your life. Keep reading this book for practical advice on how to get your money matters on track.

MOSTLY Bs

You seem to have a very healthy outlook on money matters and you certainly know its worth. You have realised that by keeping an eye on what you spend and what you save you have taken the first step towards controlling your financial future. You spend when you have to, and also make allowances for special occasions and the odd luxury. It could almost be the case that, here, B is for budgeting – ever considered a career in banking, insurance or as an accountant? You are on the right track, but keep reading this book for helpful hints and tips on making the most of your money.

MOSTLY Cs

You are definitely a spender rather than a saver, and would rather let tomorrow take care of itself while you enjoy today. This is all very well if you have the finances to cover the cost of buying the latest fashions or design trends – if you don't, you could well spend the rest of your life running to keep up with your galloping debts. You also seem to think having the newest gadget or trainers somehow enhances your worth as a person. But having money or material things won't make you nicer/more popular/brainier/more attractive. These are all attributes that come from within – you can't wear them or carry them about with you. Your devil-may-care attitude to money could land you in serious trouble, so it's time to wise up, read this book, get your finances sorted out and realise that genuine people will like you for yourself and not for your money.

'When your friends buy new things, it does make you want to have them. I've got some friends who are much richer than my family and they always have new things, and I always want what they've got.'
Isabel Rose, 13

'Without money our society would not work, but it causes stress and jealousy. It does not seem fair that some people work so hard yet get paid so little.'
Claire Gomer, 14

WHY PEOPLE SPEND MONEY

Money makes me feel good because (when I have it) I know I can buy whatever I want, whenever I want.'

Ranveer Rana, 13

The most obvious reason why people spend money is out of necessity – they need to eat and to drink, clothe themselves and have a roof over their heads, and all of that costs money. However, there are a lot of other reasons why people spend money. Read the following statements and see if you relate to any of them.

1 I spend money to make myself feel better.

Many people who have low self-esteem find spending money makes them feel better about themselves – it is as if they are saying, 'If I spend this money on myself, then I must be worth something'. However, blowing your pounds and pence is never going to fix the underlying problem: you need to start valuing yourself for yourself.

The same is true if you find yourself spending money when you are feeling blue or depressed. You are using buying things as a displacement action – 'I'm depressed so I'll buy this new CD player to take my mind off my depression.' Unfortunately, this will only ever work in the short term, because you have not addressed the root of your unhappiness. What you need to do is identify what it is you are unhappy about (family troubles/boyfriend or girlfriend problems/ bullying/exams), and then set about solving the real problem.

For a closer look at building your confidence, see *Real Life Issues: Confidence and Self-Esteem* by Nicki Household. It offers practical advice and tips on ways of acquiring a more positive outlook on life.

2 I spend money to keep up with the Joneses.

'I want the things my friends have because I do not want to feel left out.'

Chris Leonard, 14

'I get things when I want them and not just because my friends have got them.'

Linda Laryea, 14

TIP BOX

Self-esteem is all about thinking positive thoughts and giving out positive energy, so what you need to do is stop undermining your confidence with negative thoughts such as, 'I'm worthless, no one likes me, I have nothing to offer', and start thinking, 'I'm a worthwhile person, I deserve to have great friends, and I can offer them and society in general so much.'

In our modern, voraciously consumerist world being a teen can be hard. This is because all the big companies want to hook you in as a customer when you are young, and keep you loyal for life – Coca-Cola doesn't want to lose you to Pepsi, and Nike doesn't want Adidas to poach your business. Because of this, they are willing to spend billions of pounds on advertising their products, implying that if you use them you will be brighter, smarter, sexier and more attractive than if you use a rival's products. This is how certain brands become must-haves: Sarah Jessica Parker advertises Lux bath products, so I must use them too; David Beckham sports Police sunglasses so I must have a pair; Ronan Keating has an ipod, so I must buy one immediately. If you desperately want to be liked by a certain group of people you see as trendy and cool, and they all have access to these luxury goods, then the temptation is to believe that they will like you if you have these brands too. Advertising and peer pressure can be very hard to resist, but keep working on your self-esteem and confidence and you'll realise that having a Dolce e Gabbana handbag like Posh's doesn't make you a better person than the girl in your class who bought hers at Topshop (in fact, she's probably made a better purchase!).

'I wouldn't want something just because a celebrity endorsed it, but if everybody else at school had something, I would probably want it too.'

Paul Welsh, 13

3 I spend money because I just can't stop.

Like alcoholism and drug abuse, spending money can become an addiction. In some people this manifests itself as an inability to stop gambling (the rationale being 'just one more bet and I'll win a million'), in others as a rampage with a credit card that leaves them thousands of pounds in debt. The reasons for this can be many: low self-esteem and depression, as explained earlier, or an addictive personality that means a person will become addicted to one thing or another at some time. Addiction is an illness and you really need to get help as soon as you can. Your first step is to talk to someone, anyone, about your problem. ChildLine has trained, volunteer counsellors who can offer you confidential advice 24 hours a day. ChildLine is on 0800 1111 (for more information see 'Resources' at the end of this book).

> **For a closer look at these issues, see *Real Life Issues: Addictions* by Stephen Briggs. It gives honest advice and will help you to ascertain whether you really do have an addiction.**

WHY PEOPLE DON'T SPEND MONEY

'Not having much money makes me feel worried that if I need to go out and buy something, I won't be able to.'

Laura Wilson, 14

Some people don't spend money because they don't have any, others because they are natural misers, but the main reason why people who have money don't spend it is *fear*. They are afraid of money itself. This may be because they have never learned how to use it efficiently or responsibly. It may be that their family has never had a bank account or a debit card or a credit card and, like anything new, thinking about learning about these things is worse than the actual learning itself. As you will find as you read through this book, money is, most definitely, to be respected, but not to be feared. Once you get the hang of how to manage your financial transactions, you'll feel more in control of your life as a whole. Remember, money is a tool for you to use wisely. If you're ready to begin learning how, then turn to the next chapter where you'll find out what banks can do for you.

'I don't like money. It corrupts people and becomes too central to many people's lives.'

Paul Waldron, 14

'Money means responsibility.'

Abbey Hitchcock, 13

CHAPTER TWO:

TAKE IT TO THE BANK
Choosing the right bank, what banks can do for you

We've become so used to seeing banks on the high street, hearing about the profits they make in the news and reading their ads in the papers, that it's almost impossible to think of a time when banks didn't exist. However, before money had even been invented, financial transactions were taking place in the form of trade or bartering. People would exchange things they had made or found, such as shell necklaces or stone tools, for food or other staples. As trading grew, the number of necklaces or tools people had to carry around became too great, and they realised they needed some form of token they could exchange that would represent the worth of the goods or services that had been traded. Those tokens became money; however, it was still centuries after money was invented that banks came into existence.

People started to leave their money with goldsmiths and what started as the practice of depositing money and taking it out again soon became much more sophisticated, with other services, such as money lending, being offered. What we would recognise as modern banks came into existence in the seventeenth century (the Bank of England in 1694), while building societies (where workers clubbed together to buy land to build houses where they could live) started in the mid-nineteenth century. These days, both banks and building societies offer a vast range of services, including current accounts, personal loans, credit cards and insurance.

What's so good about banks?

In the modern world, we need banks and bank accounts more than ever before. Not only is it safer to have your money in a bank than stashed under your mattress, but also many of our everyday financial transactions are now automated or electronic, and actual money – in notes or coins – does not change hands. You may go into a record store and buy CDs using a Maestro card (formerly known as Switch), where the money is taken straight from your account, and your wages may well be paid by BACS (a system where funds can be transferred between banks for the settlement of payments) where the money goes straight into your account. Your bank sorts all of this out for you and provides you with statements letting you know what has come out of, and gone into, your account. Banks and building societies also offer savings accounts where you can deposit money with them and earn regular interest on what you have saved (this is dealt with in more detail in Chapter 5, 'Saving For A Rainy Day'), and this means that your money is working harder for you. So, if you haven't got a bank account already, you should really start thinking about getting one.

CHOOSING THE RIGHT BANK

Many people choose a bank for the most simple of reasons – it's the bank their mum and dad use. Josie Clapham of HSBC says:

'Parental recommendation can be so key in this market. Young people are persuaded by the way their parents may bank, or because their grandparents or godparents have opened an account for them with a particular bank. It can have a very persuasive effect on where that young person will also take their banking.'

If your parents have never had any problems with their bank, all well and good; they may even have built up a good relationship with their local branch manager. But just think about it for a second. Your mum and dad may have been with this bank for years, and banking is a rapidly moving business – there may well be a bank around now that didn't exist when your parents opened their account and it could offer you services that are more geared to your needs – an Internet bank, for example.

Banking Services

The first thing to do is to choose a bank that offers all the services *you* want. Some banks and bank accounts are not available to people under

TIP BOX

You don't have to use the same bank as your parents do. It's just the same as saying that because your parents have shopped at the same store for years and years doesn't mean that their styles will suit you. You're not saying there is anything wrong with what they wear, it's just that you want to choose something that is more your style. So really think hard before coming to a decision.

the age of 18, but the good news is that many high street banks offer special young people or student accounts, with added benefits (there is a list of banks with contact details in the 'Resources' section). Things you should consider when choosing a bank and a specific account include:

- Does the current account give you interest on your money?
- Is there a debit card such as a Maestro/Delta/Switch card?
- Is there an overdraft facility and how much does it cost?
- Does the bank or account operate a telephone or Internet banking service?
- What rate of interest do you get on the savings account?
- Is there a branch with a cashpoint machine within easy access of where you live?
- Does your local branch open on Saturday?
- What other services does it offer?

The Guardian Unlimited Money website has a brilliant 'Compare And Buy' section where you can look at exactly what all the high street banks have to offer: it even lists all the banks that have student and young people accounts. Go to www.guardian.co.uk/money/compareandbuy (there is more information on the Guardian Unlimited Money website in 'Resources').

Ethical banks

If ethical issues (such as the environment and exploitation of the Third World) are important to you and you try to live your life in an ethical way, you will probably want an ethical bank. These will only buy stocks and shares in companies that are ethically sound (i.e. do not deal arms to Third World countries). On the high street, the best-known bank with ethical financial services is the Co-operative, and you can find a list of other ethical banks and building societies in the 'Resources' section.

Internet banks

Internet banking is now very popular and there are two main types of Internet bank. If you like the idea of going into the local branch of your bank, but also having the option of Internet banking, most of the high street banks now offer cyberbranches which you can gain access to by registering and being issued with an ID and password. However, there are also standalone Internet banks, such as Smile, Egg and Cahoot, which operate only on the Internet. Some provide high rates of interest on both their savings and current accounts because their overheads are kept to a minimum; however, you may find yourself being charged if you have to contact them by phone.

Types of accounts

Once you've decided on a bank, you must decide what type of account you want. Do you want a current account or a savings account? If you want both, do you want the accounts with offset interest (where the accounts are separate but positive balances in both are offset against any borrowings you may have)? What about a sweeper account where you can set an upper limit on your current account and, as soon as the amount in the account goes above this, it is automatically transferred (swept) into your savings account? Most banks can give advice on which of their products is best for your own financial circumstances, so it pays to do some research before putting them in charge of your hard-earned cash!

OPENING A BANK ACCOUNT

Once you've made up your mind, it is time to actually open an account. Don't panic! This is much easier to do than you may think and, if you have any difficulties, a banking assistant will be more than happy to help (remember, your custom is valuable to the bank). In order to set an account up for you, your bank will need certain information. You can either fill in a form or talk directly to a customer services officer at your branch. They will ask for:

- Your full name, your age (some banks will ask for parental consent for you to open an account if you are under a certain age) and your address. You will have to provide some form of ID and proof of your address (this could be a passport, your birth certificate and a bill with your address on it).
- They may ask if you have any regular sources of money coming in (in order to work out your credit scoring).
- They may ask if you want any extras along with the account, such as a cash card (if you are over 11).
- If you are 16 or over, you may be asked whether or not you want a chequebook to go with the account.
- They may ask if you wish to set up a standing order to make regular payments (such as for board and lodging) to an individual or company.
- They will ask how often you wish to receive statements (most people decide on a monthly statement).
- Finally, they will ask for an example of your signature for their records and also to be able to check against.

READING A BANK STATEMENT

Your bank statements show every transaction made either from or to your account during a specific time period (usually a month) and keeping an eye on them is very important, as they will immediately show you the state of your finances. You can see if payments have come in, what money has gone out, and how much interest (if any)

has been paid on the account. Figure 2.1 below shows a typical
example of a statement, with an explanation of what it all means.

MyBANK
STATEMENT OF ACCOUNT

SORTCODE: 00-11-22
ACCOUNT NUMBER: 12345678

26 JULY TO 27 AUGUST 2004

YOUR CURRENT ACCOUNT DETAILS

DATE	PAYMENT TYPE AND DETAILS	PAID OUT	PAID IN	BALANCE
Balance brought forward				£50.00
31 JUL	ATM MyBANK	£10		£40.00
2 AUG	DD VIRGIN MOBILE	£15		£25.00
3 AUG	INTERNAL TRANSFER	£40.00		£65.00
5 AUG	CR PAID IN MyBANK		£200	£265.00
10 AUG	ATM MyBANK	£100		£165.00
15 AUG	SWT HMV	£45		£120.00
20 AUG	1234	£100		£20.00
22 AUG	SO KEEPFIT GYM	£40		OD £20.00

Figure 2.1 A bank statement

What it all means

At the top left-hand side of the statement you will find the **sortcode**, which is the code of your particular branch of MyBANK. Every bank branch has its own unique sortcode.

Below this is your **Account Number**. Every account you have – current or savings – has its own unique number. This is so the bank can differentiate between accounts.

The **date** shows the time span for this statement and, subsequently, the dates down the left-hand side of the statement tell you which days you made certain transactions.

The **balance** of £50 at the top of the right-hand column tells you that you had £50 in your account on the date this statement started (26 July).

After that you made the following transactions:

31 July: you used an ATM (automated teller machine), or cashpoint, to take out £10 from your account.

2 August: you paid your Virgin mobile phone bill of £15 by direct debit (DD). A direct debit is where you have an agreement with a third party to claim money from your account. The amount can vary or stay the same (for example, an insurance policy).

3 August: as you were getting short of funds, you transferred £40 into your current account from your savings account. This was an internal transfer where you instructed your bank to move the money across by

Internet banking.

5 August: you paid your wages of £200 into your account by using your paying-in book at your local branch. This has shown up as a CR or credit.

15 August: you spent £45 in HMV on CDs and you paid for them by using your Switch card (SWT).

20 August: the number 1234 is the number of a cheque you wrote out for £100 to pay your mum back the money you owed her.

22 August: your regular payment to your local gym came out of your account by standing order (SO). This is where you instruct your bank to pay a specific sum of money regularly into another account. The amount remains the same. The £40 that went out on 22 August makes you £20 overdrawn (OD).

OVERDRAFT FACILITIES

An overdraft happens when more money goes out of your account than you actually have in it. Many banks now operate accounts where there is an overdraft facility already built into the account, for example of £500. That means if you go overdrawn up to £500, the bank will not charge you a fee (on most student current accounts they will also charge no interest as long as you stay within your overdraft limit). You can also set up an **agreed overdraft** with your bank, where you come to an agreement as to the extent of the overdraft. Some banks will charge you an agreement fee for this facility, others won't. If you exceed your agreed overdraft limit, the overdraft is considered **unauthorised**, and you will have to pay an excess overdraft fee as well as the agreement fee and overdraft interest. This can very quickly mount up. Many unauthorised overdrafts cost a monthly fee of £20, while interest is very high at about 30 per cent a year, and so it is best not to go overdrawn – another reason why it is so important to read your bank statements.

OTHER BANK CHARGES

As long as you stay in credit there should be no charge for your bank account; however, overdrafts aren't the only charges you can incur at the bank. Some banks will charge for extra copies of statements, although the fee is quite small. If you stop a cheque (ask the bank not to pay a cheque you have written), it will cost you £10, but it is even more expensive if you write a cheque which then bounces (i.e. you do not have enough money in your account to pay the amount of the cheque). In this case, the bank returns the cheque and charges you £30.

By now, you should understand more about what banks actually do, and below you will find a glossary of much of the jargon attached to the banking industry. In the following chapter, we will explore the paraphernalia attached to banking – all the cards, paying-in books and chequebooks – so you'll have more idea of what goes on outside of the bank as well as in it.

BANKING JARGON

ATM (automated teller machine)
Not only can you withdraw cash from ATMs (or **cashpoints** as they are commonly known), but you can also check your balance, order statements and, in some cases, even order new chequebooks.

BALANCE
The amount of money you have in your account.

DIRECT DEBIT
Where you make an agreement with a third party to pay out money to them regularly. The amount can change or stay the same.

OVERDRAFT
Where you have spent more money than you have in your account. You can agree an overdraft facility with your bank.

STANDING ORDER
Where you instruct your bank to pay a certain amount of money regularly to an organisation. The amount remains the same.

THE BANKING CODE

The Banking Code is subscribed to by many banks, building societies and financial services providers in this country, so when choosing your bank make sure you ask whether it follows the Banking Code. The Code covers everything from dealing with customers' complaints quickly and effectively to helping to sort out financial difficulties, and protecting customers' accounts and all their personal information. It ensures that customers are provided with information in clear language that they can understand easily and that they are given the best help to make the right financial decisions for their own personal circumstances.

The Banking Code ensures that:
- products meet the relevant laws and regulations
- banking systems are safe and reliable
- all the bank's services and products meet the Code standards
- the bank treats those suffering financial difficulties positively and sympathetically.

However, if and when things do go wrong, the Code specifies that:
- mistakes will be dealt with quickly
- complaints will be handled quickly
- bank charges that have been incurred because of a mistake (a direct debit going out twice, a cancelled standing order still being paid) will be paid back in full.

(For a full copy of the Banking Code go to the British Bankers' Association website at www.bba.org.uk.)

CHAPTER THREE:

WHAT'S IN YOUR WALLET?
Cheques, cards, statements...

While new technologies have largely bypassed the need to carry actual coins and notes around in our pockets, our wallets and purses are just as stuffed these days as ever, but now with chequebooks, cheque guarantee cards, credit cards, debit cards, loyalty cards and store cards. Sometimes it becomes confusing knowing what they are all for, but once their use has been mastered, they can make your money matters much easier (as long as you use them responsibly!).

CHEQUEBOOKS

Let's start with the oldest technology listed above, the **chequebook** and **cheque guarantee card**. Although still a useful tool to help you handle your finances, cheques are quickly being overtaken by the newer technologies. In many shops, only a tiny minority of transactions will now involve the filling out of a cheque, as people prefer to use credit and debit cards. However, if you want to send someone money by post (as payment for goods or as a birthday present), then a cheque is a safe way to do so. The dummy cheque, Figure 3.1 below, will not only show you the main features but will also explain how to fill out a cheque correctly.

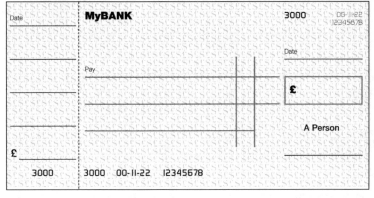

Figure 3.1 A dummy cheque

What it all means

The blank left-hand side of the cheque before the perforations is known as the cheque **counterfoil.** Here, you should write down the details of the cheque (the date you are writing it, who you are making it out to, and how much it is for).

The number 3000 at the bottom of the counterfoil and also at the top right of the cheque and bottom left of the cheque is the **cheque number**. Each of your cheques has its own individual number. When you come to read your statement you will be able to see which of the cheques you have written have actually gone through the clearance system by checking the cheque numbers. It takes three days for a cheque to clear. This means that it will take three days from the time it is deposited at a bank until the money appears in the account of the payee (person the cheque is made out to).

The sequence of figures '00–11–22' is your bank sortcode. This is the code for your own particular bank.

The long number 12345678 is your bank account number. This will tell the payee's bank which account the money must be withdrawn from.

The box with the pound sign in it is where you write out the amount payable on the cheque in numbers.

Below this box it says 'A Person'. This is the name of the account holder and the cheque must be signed directly under this.

FILLING OUT A CHEQUE

The trick to writing cheques is to concentrate while you are doing it because if you get distracted you can make mistakes, and these can mean the cheque will be rejected.

Date

To start off with, write the date in the appropriate space. This is important because if you try to cash a cheque that is over six months old, or one that has been **post dated** (made out for a date in the future), it will be rejected.

Who the cheque is for

You must put the full name of the individual or company the cheque is for on the cheque. For example, your best mate may be called Jill Smith, but if her bank account is in the name of Ms Gillian Smith and you make out a cheque to her in the name 'Jill Smith', it may be rejected.

The amount

Many people combine letters and numbers when they write out cheques, e.g.

Pay Ms Gillian Smith ten pounds and 52 pence only ——————

(The 'only' and the line are so you use up all the space on the cheque so no one can alter the amount.)

Letters and numbers are fine *as long as* the amount you write on the body of the cheque agrees with the amount you write in the box.

Your signature

Finally, you need to sign your cheque, and you have to make sure your signature agrees with the name printed on the cheque (see above).

Always write your cheques out in pen, not pencil, and if you do make a mistake, you must initial or sign any alterations you make. Make sure you don't leave spaces where people could add or otherwise change the figures on the cheque.

The cheque guarantee card

In order to use your chequebook, you will also need a cheque guarantee card, which 'guarantees' your bank will honour any cheques you make out up to a certain amount (the limit is usually £100). These days most debit cards also act as cheque guarantee cards (see below). When you receive your card, you must sign it immediately.

This is because the card acts as an extra safety check for the retailer, who makes sure the signatures on the cheque and card tally before accepting the cheque as payment. If the cheque is accepted and honoured by your bank, but you do not have enough funds in your account to cover the amount of the cheque, then you may incur charges.

The retailer will check that:
- the signatures on the cheque and cheque card are identical (This is most important because one or other could be stolen)
- your signature has not rubbed off or become illegible
- the card is not out of date
- the limit of the card (usually £100) covers the amount on the cheque
- the card does not appear on the register of stolen cards.

There is a box on card security at the end of this chapter.

Finally, *always* keep a note of what cheques you have made out, for how much and to whom. This is why the cheque counterfoils (sometimes known as stubs) are included in your chequebook. There

FACT BOX

Banks won't issue chequebooks to under-16-year-olds but, if and when you do get a chequebook and guarantee card, remember to keep them both safe but not in the same place. If either the chequebook or card goes missing, advise your bank and the police immediately.

is nothing more annoying than to look at your statement and see a cheque has cleared and not have the foggiest idea what it was for.

Now let's take a look at **debit cards** which you may know as **cash cards** or under the names of **Maestro, Switch** or **Delta cards**.

DEBIT CARDS

You can go a long way and do a lot of things with a debit card. For example, you can use it instead of cash or cheques in shops, over the phone or on the Internet. You can use it as a cheque guarantee card (see above), to deposit money, to get cashback, check the balance of your account and even order a new chequebook electronically. You can also use it to withdraw cash 24 hours a day from cashpoint machines across the country, and in some cases even abroad. When you first get your card you will be given a four-digit **PIN** (Personal Identification Number) that you will need in order to withdraw cash from ATMs. You will be able to change the number the first time you use the card in a machine to something you know you won't forget.

Basically, every time you use your debit card, the amount of the transaction is immediately withdrawn from your bank account. If you don't have the money in your account, the transaction will be refused (unless you have an agreed overdraft facility). The great thing about this is that you can't spend what you have not got which, along with interest payments, is the main difference between a debit card and a credit card.

Here are some examples of how you can use your card:
■ You are going to the cinema with some friends. On the way you stop at an ATM to withdraw £20 and, while there, you ask for the balance of your account to be displayed on the screen. You see you are still £43.53 in credit after withdrawing the money.

■ You've gone into Boots to buy some toiletries, and the final bill is £15.99. You want to pay by debit card so you give the assistant your card, which she then swipes through the machine. If the card is accepted, she will give you a receipt to sign. If your signature on the debit card and the signature on the receipt match, she will give you one copy of the receipt while retaining the other copy.

■ You've bought some items at Safeway and when you get to the checkout you produce your Maestro card. The assistant asks if you want to get cashback and you say, 'Yes, £20 please'. The assistant adds the cashback amount to the total and then swipes the card through the machine. You sign the receipt for the goods plus cashback (initialling the cashback amount), and then the assistant gives you one copy of the receipt, plus two £10 notes.

Chip and PIN

There are currently changes happening to debit cards. Rather than using the card and signature method, Britain is in the process of swapping to the **Chip and PIN** debit cards favoured in Europe. With Chip and PIN you do not sign the receipt but, once the card has gone through a reading machine, you key in your PIN. This is a much more secure method than relying on signatures because, in the event of your card being stolen, only you should know your PIN. The minimum age for having a debit card depends on your particular bank or building society, so do check (in some cases you will need parental approval).

CREDIT CARDS

Many people also have **credit cards** tucked away in their wallets. Credit cards are one of the easiest ways of borrowing money over a short period; however, they can prove to be a very expensive way of borrowing. As with debit cards, you can use them both to withdraw cash from ATMs and to purchase goods. As with a debit card, you will be given a spending limit; however, unlike debit cards the money does not come straight out of your account. Instead, each month you will receive a statement listing the transactions you have made with the credit card over that period (and any outstanding balance, if there is any). You then have the option to either pay off the amount in full or to pay a part of the amount.

If you pay the amount in full you are not charged interest; however, if you only pay off part of the amount, you will be charged interest on the amount left. On most cards, the minimum amount you can pay is £5 or 5 per cent of the balance, so if you owe £200, the minimum payment would be £10. If you pay that £10, you will have to pay interest on the £190 you still owe, and if you pay late or not at all, you will be charged a penalty fee (penalty fees can be in the region of £24). If you exceed your limit you can also be charged a penalty fee. You need to check what **APR** (annual percentage rate) each credit card company charges because they can vary greatly. Basically, you are looking for the lowest APR you can find. Some credit card companies also charge an annual fee for the privilege of having the card, so look for one that doesn't.

Do you really need a credit card?

You have to be 18 to apply for a credit card, and with good reason: if they are not used responsibly they can get you into serious trouble. Spending on 'plastic', as it is called, is so easy that some people get addicted to it. This is when problems can really arise because people spend and spend up to their limit and, if they only pay the minimum each month, the interest owed really starts to mount up. Getting into bad debt on your credit card is not something you want to do (see Chapter 6, 'Money's Too Tight To Mention'), so if you think you may be tempted to overspend on plastic, take some time to think about whether you really need a credit card or not. Ask yourself why you are getting one. If it is because all your friends have got one, you may be giving in to peer pressure. It is hard when you seem to be the odd person out, but if you only have limited funds, a debit card – where you can only spend what you actually have in your account – may be a better bet for you. Also, if you know you have a habit of impulse buying, then a credit card may be more of a temptation than you can resist. Remove the temptation by not getting a credit card but opening a savings account instead, then if you see something you really, really want to buy you will have the satisfaction of knowing you have enough funds saved to pay for it outright.

> *'Work with cash and debit cards. Get rid of the credit cards completely: there lies a path of destruction!'*
>
> **Emma B, presenter, BBC Radio 1's *Sunday Surgery* advice show for young people**

Many credit card firms are now updating their cards to the Chip and PIN format for security reasons.

Charge cards, such as American Express, are different from credit cards because you have to pay the balance of your account off on a monthly basis. Most charge a joining fee and an annual subscription.

Store Cards act like credit cards for specific companies (for example, Debenhams, Topshop, Marks & Spencer) and, although you may initially get special offers for joining the scheme, once again, if you do not pay your balance off in full, you can end up getting charged extremely high levels of interest (at the time of writing the IKEA card was charging a hefty 29 per cent APR). Although the Office of Fair Trading (OFT) records that one in three adults now has a store card, once again you should ask yourself if you really, really need one or if it would be better for you to stick with your debit card and only buy goods when you can actually afford them. The OFT is so concerned about store cards that it has produced a leaflet entitled *Are You Store Card Smart*? You can obtain a copy from the OFT website at www.oft.gov.uk and from 0870 6060321.

So, here's a quick checklist of what you may have in your wallet and what it is good for:

■ **Cheque and cheque guarantee card**. Good for sending money by post and for using in shops and stores or if you want to give a payment to family and friends (maybe as a birthday present or paying off a debt) but don't want to do so in cash.

■ **Debit cards**. A very useful alternative to having actual cash in your pocket. Use them to withdraw money from ATMs, check balances, order statements, make deposits, pay for goods and get cashback.

■ **Credit cards**. Useful for buying goods without cash, but make sure you pay your balance off each month, otherwise the interest and other charges can quickly get out of hand. If you think you may be tempted to overspend with a credit card, *don't get one*.

■ **Store cards**. Just like credit cards they will charge you interest if you don't pay the entire balance off each month. It is better to save up and buy the things you want when you know you have the funds to pay for them.

In the next chapter, we will look in detail at how you can regulate money coming in and going out of your current account or savings. Being sensible with money may not seem very sexy, but it will save you from the very real headaches associated with getting into debt and living in poverty. Remember: with so many people wanting to lend you money these days, it is very easy to rack up a large debt very quickly, but it is much more difficult to pay that debt off again.

KEEPING YOUR CARDS SAFE

Carrying a credit or debit card around with you is safer than carrying cash, but you do need to follow a few simple rules in order to protect your card.

Your pin

■ When you first get your debit card (or one of the new Chip and PIN cards), you will be issued with a PIN of four digits that you can easily change the first time you use the card, if you don't think you are going to be able to remember it.

■ There are some numbers you can't choose for security reasons (like a run of 3333 or 6666), and you should choose something memorable to you that will easily come to mind, although it is best not to choose a year such as 1999. Don't give your PIN to anyone else, however. Because of the increase in card fraud, it is a good idea to keep a record of your PIN and your card account number, but keep them separately in sealed envelopes.

All cards

■ Sign your card as soon as it is in your possession and from time to time make sure your signature hasn't rubbed off or become otherwise illegible.

■ Try not to keep all your cards together in the same place in your purse or wallet because this can corrupt the special strip on the back of the card that is read when the card is swiped (i.e. run through the machine at the till).

■ Make sure the card does not get bent or too scratched as this can also corrupt the card.

Statements

■ Always open your credit or store card statements the moment they arrive because you need to check to see that the purchases they say you have made, you actually have made. If there are discrepancies, check you still have your card in your possession. If you do still have your card, then it could be your card has been cloned, i.e. someone has made a forged card with your details on it and is making fraudulent transactions using your account. Once again, immediately ring the emergency number. The sooner the card provider is informed, the sooner they can stop money being taken from your account illegally.

■ If you don't have your card, then you must immediately contact your card issuer to report it stolen or lost, as the sooner it is cancelled the less chance there is that you will be liable for any purchases made. All the major credit card providers have emergency numbers you can call.*

■ If you are sure the card has been stolen, report it to the police and obtain a crime reference number.

*A list of these numbers is contained in the 'Resources' section.

RATE TARTS

There are so many credit card companies around these days, all vying for your custom, that some offer a special incentive for you to switch to them. Basically, if you transfer the balance from your old card to these new cards, they will charge you 0% interest for a specific amount of time (usually between six months and one year).

If you are finding it difficult to keep up with your card repayments, then this can seem a very attractive solution in the short term – as you are not paying interest, it gives you a breathing space in which to pay off the balance of the account. In fact, the term 'Rate Tart' has now been coined for people who keep moving their balances between cards to take advantage of these 0% interest offers.

Beware!

If you have a troublesome debt, this may seem like the answer to all your prayers, but at some point you are going to have to start paying interest, so *check what the APR is before you sign on*. You may find it is going to be higher than the APR charged on your original card. You may also find that if you don't pay the minimum payments on the card on time you lose the 0% interest offer and have to start paying interest anyway. As ever, check the small print, and if you are in any doubt, *don't do it*!

CHAPTER FOUR:

BALANCING THE BOOKS
Knowing where your money goes

'Having money means having to budget.'

Laura Wilson, 14

It's interesting to note that the word that we use to describe a sense of harmony in our lives is also the word we use when describing our financial status. In both cases we talk about a state of balance. When all aspects of our personal lives are balanced, we feel at peace with ourselves and can cope with any emotional challenges we face; when our finances are balanced, we don't have to worry about them, and can conserve our energies for more productive purposes, such as earning more money! In this chapter, we will explore how you can keep your financial affairs in balance (known as balancing the books) so you can concentrate on important things like searching for the ideal career, finding somewhere to live, getting that all-important job and basically enjoying your life.

Keeping tabs on your money

If you are not particularly mathematically minded, thinking about keeping tabs on all your financial transactions and the numbers they

generate may seem like an impossible task. Once again, don't panic!
In fact, it is a very simple equation: you subtract all your outgoings
from the money you have coming in, and what is left is the balance.
Sometimes you will have money left over, sometimes you will find you
have spent more than you have earned and so are in debt – but at
least you know by how much.

With a little self-discipline, and a few minutes spent each day or each
week, balancing your books will become second nature. The trick is to
break the task down into easy pieces:

■ The first thing to do is to decide on the time span that your budget
will cover. You can break it down into separate weeks or separate
months, but you can't mix the two because it will upset the

FACT BOX

*The reason why so many people
get into financial difficulties is that
they don't keep track of their
money. This is a stupid state of
affairs to get into. Money is a
precious commodity, and you
want to know where every penny
of your hard-earned cash goes.
Billionaire John Paul Getty was so
aware of the value of money that
when he discovered one of his
managers had bought an electric
pencil sharpener, he made him
take it back and return to a
cheaper manual one instead.*

numbers. For the examples here, we will be working on a weekly budget.

■ The next thing to remember is to keep all your cheque stubs, paying-in slips and receipts from cash transactions and any other sources (credit or debit cards and even from taking money from ATMs). Not only does this make sense security wise, but also there's nothing worse than looking at your bank statement at the end of the month and discovering you had withdrawn £50 more from cash machines than you had remembered. That £50 could put you into the red, incurring bank charges.

■ Then you need to calculate how much your income amounts to. Remember to include everything you earn. You may get income from a Saturday job or babysitting, you may be working part time in a bar while you study, you may have a student grant, or you may be given an allowance by your parents. The total is the amount you have to spend a week.

■ Now you need to add up all your expenditures – that is, everything you have going out of your account. Put the amounts that are fixed, or paid out regularly, first. These will be rent (if you pay any), utilities such as water, electricity and gas (if you pay for these), your mobile phone bill, any repayments on loans or credit cards, transport (including car tax and insurance if you have a car), regular newspaper or magazine subscriptions, food and clothing (including regular mail-order payments) and any regular savings you make. Next, add on incidentals, such as money you have spent on going out, on make-up, on CDs or DVDs, on birthday presents and even on holidays.

■ To work out the balance you simply subtract the outgoing total from the incoming total. The easiest way to do this is in a chart like the one below.

MY WEEKLY OUTGOINGS

	WEEK ONE	WEEK TWO
INCOME		
ALLOWANCE	£20	£20
SATURDAY JOB	£25	£25
BIRTHDAY MONEY		£150
MONEY BOB OWED ME	£10	
TOTAL	£55	£195
OUTGOINGS		
TRAVEL	£10	£10
SAVINGS	£5	£5
MAGAZINES	£6	£6
MOBILE PHONE	£5	£5
COSTA COFFEE	£3	£5
NEW SHOES		£35
CINEMA TRIP		£12
TOTAL	£29	£78
BALANCE	(£55 – £29 = £26)	(£195 – £78 = £117)
	£26	£117

Figure 4.1 A balance sheet

This balance sheet is obviously for someone who does not yet have a full-time job, does not earn that much money and is pretty good about spending. When they eventually leave school and get a full-time job or go to college they will earn more, but expenditures will also increase. Most people's incomes start quite low and get higher with annual pay rises as they gain more experience, switch jobs or get promoted. What also tends to happen is that as people earn and spend more, they also tend to save more so they complete dozens of transactions a week. Keeping track of their money then becomes even more important.

'Having money makes me feel comfortable, but just because I have it, doesn't mean I have to spend it.'

Linda Laryea, 14

YOUR FIRST JOB

When you finally do get that all-important first full-time job, you may get a shock when you look at your first wage slip (a statement of what you have earned and any deductions made). What a lot of people *never* budget for in their balances is the fact that, if you are employed by a company, you will probably be **PAYE** (Pay As You Earn), where you will be charged income tax and National Insurance (NI), and these will be deducted at source (i.e. by your employer before the money gets to you). The process is different if you are self-employed although, even if you work for yourself, you must make allowances for tax and NI contributions. Income tax is what we pay to the government to fund public services such as new road schemes, hospitals, schools and the infrastructure that keeps our society going. National Insurance

pays for sickness benefits and state pensions (for more information
see the box at the end of this chapter). When you first start to work
you should estimate losing roughly 25 per cent of your pay (so if you
are on £1,000 per month gross, what you will actually get is £750 net
– the gross minus deductions). Below is an example of a wage slip
and how to read it.

A COMPANY	SALARY	DEDUCTIONS	AMOUNT
MR A SMITH TOPS HILL LEEDS N.I. AB123456C	£1256.75	NI PAYE PENSION SCHEME	£ 86.62 £ 220.52 £ 29.75
		GROSS PAY	£ 1256.75
		TOTAL DEDUCTIONS	£ 336.89
		NET PAY	£ 919.86

Figure 4.2 A wage slip

This tells us that A. Smith (National Insurance number AB123456C)
works for a business called A Company and his monthly salary is
£1,256.75. From this is deducted National Insurance (£86.62) and
income tax (£220.52). We also know that Mr Smith has been sensible
enough to join A Company's pension scheme, and so £29.75 from his
wages goes straight into his pension each month. After these amounts
have been taken out, Mr Smith gets a total of £919.86 per month
paid into his account via the BACS system.

'I've applied for a Sunday job in retail. I think this is not only extremely useful for when I apply for jobs in the future, but will also be good as it gives me a supply of money that is purely my own.'

Alice-Lara Waterman, 16

TIPPING THE BALANCE IN YOUR FAVOUR

Now you've seen how it all works, the thing to do is to think about ways you can balance the books so they are more in your favour. Of course, getting a better-paid job or a second job will immediately increase your income, but this is not always possible. It may be feasible to find ways to cut down on your outgoings. Here are a few things you should think about:

■ Your mobile phone. Take a good hard look at the tariff for your phone. Would you be able to get a better deal elsewhere? If so, then seriously consider switching to the better deal. If not, think about ways you can make savings on your calls. Never call during peak hours, and just think how much each text message is costing you – they may only cost a few pence each, perhaps 3p, but if you text ten friends ten times each a day that is £3 you've spent on messages that might only be two words long. Think before you press that send button!

■ Transport. If you regularly use the bus/tube/train it pays to save for a weekly or monthly ticket because this is cheaper than individual tickets each day. Also, see if it is viable to either cycle or walk on some journeys you are currently paying to make.

■ Buy clothes in the sales. At present there is a huge price war going on in the high street, with every retailer trying to increase its share of the profits. This means you will find bargains galore, including wonderful savings during the big seasonal sales. In some cases, you will find prices slashed by as much as 50 per cent. Canny shoppers know to wait a few weeks after the new season's stock has arrived in the shops, and then to pounce when it is all reduced in the sale.

■ If you have to buy your own food look for supermarket own brands and special '2 for 1' offers.

■ If you have to pay your own utility bills then pay them promptly. Most utility providers now offer a prompt payment discount, meaning the quicker you pay, the less the bill is.

■ If you do have surplus cash at the end of each week or month then make sure you put it into a savings account. This will not cut down on your outgoings, but a savings account will pay you interest and so make your money work harder for you (see Chapter 5, 'Saving For A Rainy Day').

■ *Don't* incur bank charges by going over your overdraft limit without consulting the bank first. This is just throwing money away needlessly. Keep your bank informed and come to an agreement.

■ *Don't* build up huge amounts of interest on a credit card. Again, this is just throwing money away. If you do have to have a credit card, then make sure you budget to pay off the balance each and every month (you can do so by organising a direct debit from your account).

NATIONAL INSURANCE: WHAT IS IT?

National Insurance is the money taken out of your wages to entitle you to benefits such as Incapacity Benefit and the basic State Pension. The amount you pay will depend on your employment status. For example, if you are self-employed, or are being awarded benefit credits, your contributions will be different from someone in full-time employment. In order for the Inland Revenue to track your National Insurance Contributions (NIC), you are given a National Insurance number, and you will keep that same number all your life.

NI numbers consist of two letters, followed by six numbers, followed by one letter A, B, C. For example:

AB234567C

The Inland Revenue National Insurance Contributions Office issues NI numbers to those approaching 16 years of age and to those who are working or claiming benefit. If you do not have a NI number you should contact your nearest Jobcentre Plus office and tell them the situation. They can interview you for one. To find out where your nearest Jobcentre Plus office is go to www.jobcentreplus.gov.uk and click on 'About Us' on the home page. Then click on 'Our Offices'.

More information about applying for a NI number can be found on the Department For Work and Pensions' website: www.dwp.gov.uk.

For detailed information on National Insurance and tax issues in general, check out the Inland Revenue website at www.inlandrevenue.gov.uk.

CHAPTER FIVE:

SAVING FOR A RAINY DAY
Making your money grow

'If you don't learn to save you'll never learn the value of money.'
Nick Sahota, 13

You're young, with your whole future ahead of you, and you want to have fun before adult responsibilities, such as marriage, children and a mortgage get in the way. You may think that saving also belongs in the future, but there are some very good reasons for getting into the habit of saving from an early age. In fact, according to a survey carried out by BBC TV's *Shortchange* programme, 58 per cent of young people are keen to save their money, and it makes good sense for them to do so. You may be saving for something special – the trip of a lifetime, a scooter – or for going away to college, or you may even be saving for something further in the future – such as the deposit for a flat.

A recent Marks & Spencer 'Money' survey found that 56 per cent of people were saving for a holiday, 27 per cent were saving up to buy a car, a further 27 per cent were saving towards a deposit for a house and 18 per cent were saving for a shopping spree. These are all really good reasons for saving, but there is a more basic reason, and that is it makes your money work harder for you. Savings accounts pay you interest on your money. If you were to just put your money in a piggy bank, it would actually decrease in value over the years because of inflation (each year the cost of living rises, so your money buys you less). However, if you put your money in a high-interest account, the value of your money increases faster than inflation, and so your money will actually buy you more.

'The first large item I ever saved up for was my first car, a Ford KA. I was so proud of it and so excited that I had saved for it and it was all mine.'

Emma B, presenter, BBC Radio 1 *Sunday Surgery*

'It's alright being given money but it is more rewarding if you earn it by having a job. I deliver newspapers and have to get up at six every morning but it's worth it. That's how I saved up for my trampoline, and the next thing I'm buying is a tennis racquet.' **Paul Welsh, 13**

Spending habits of British teenagers

According to a recent report by Mintel, British children between the ages of 7 and 14 receive a massive £1.5 billion in pocket money, while those between the ages of 15 and 16 receive a further £1.6

billion, meaning the total spending power of 7 to 16-year-olds is over £3 billion. That's a lot of cash to be spending on goods and going out. It's also a lot of cash that could potentially be saved. What the report found, however, was that it was younger children who were more careful with their money. Almost 60 per cent of 7- to 10-year-olds said they actually enjoyed saving money compared to just 45 per cent of 11- to 16-year-olds. Also, 40 per cent of older children said they spent money without thinking.

Jenny Catlin, consumer analyst at Mintel, says:

'A main influence on children and teens' changing spending habits results from the phenomenon of kids growing older younger. Today, children tend to emulate adult behaviour at a younger age than they did in previous generations. Research shows that older children have a looser attitude towards savings and debt, a trait that we see only too often amongst adults today. Older children tend to spend and enjoy their money, and a smaller proportion of teens save, compared to their younger counterparts.'

Saving, however, is really important. It's not just that you can save to buy the things you really want, but getting into the habit of saving means you will be able to regulate your spending more effectively in the future.

STARTING TO SAVE

If you want to start saving, the first thing you have to do is work out how much you can actually afford to save. Will you be able to put away a specific amount each week or month? Or will you only be able to save periodically as money comes in (birthday gifts, or wages from odd jobs)? Once you know how you want to save, you need to find a savings account or plan that works for you. As stated previously, most of the high street banks now offer savings accounts specifically geared to young people. Many offer gift tokens, cash presents, free vouchers or other incentives for you to take out an account with them. These may seem attractive, but much more important is what the bank or building society can offer you in the long run.

Make sure you ask the following questions:
- Will I be able to withdraw money from the account immediately, or will I have to give a certain amount of notice?
- Can money be withdrawn using ATMs?
- Is there a local branch within easy distance of where I live?
- Is there a minimum sum I must deposit in order to open the account?
- What is the rate of interest you give on savings? (This is very important – you are looking to get the best APR you can.)

Once again, check out the *Guardian*'s excellent 'Compare and Buy' website that shows exactly what all the major bank and building society savings accounts can offer you:
www.guardian.co.uk/money/compareandbuy.

Opening a savings account

Once you have made your choice, opening a savings account is easy. First of all, contact your local branch and tell them you wish to open an account. They will give you an application form to fill out (ask an assistant to help you if you are unsure of what to do). When you return the application you will have to show some form of identification, such as your passport or birth certificate, and also proof of your address (utility bills such as gas or electric bills will do). You

'The first expensive item I can remember saving for was my elective training at medical school. This is when you spend time working in a hospital anywhere in the world to help broaden your experience – I chose Trinidad and Tobago. It took the best part of a year to save up enough spends. However, things were quite cheap out there, so the money went a long way!'

Dr Mark Hamilton, presenter, Radio 1's *Sunday Surgery*

will then have to give them an example of your signature for future identification and make your first deposit.

Take a look at the 'Resources' section at the back of this book. There you will find a list of the major banks and building societies, with details of their accounts for young people.

National savings accounts

You can also save at the Post Office. National Savings are administered through the Post Office and give good rates of interest. Ask at your local branch for details.

A savings account is not the only way you can make your money work for you. The government and financial bodies are becoming increasingly worried that people are not saving enough for their long-term future, i.e. for their retirement. Apparently only one in five people is taking a long-term view of their savings.

Personal pensions and stakeholder pensions

Introduced in April 2001, stakeholder pensions are now taking over from personal pensions as the long-term savings choice for most people. This is because charges (for administering the plan) on stakeholder pensions are capped at just 1 per cent, while the charges on personal pensions can be as much as 2.5 per cent. You can take your stakeholder pension with you when you change jobs and there are no surrender penalties (some personal pensions will charge a fee if you close the plan prematurely). You can also keep a stakeholder pension going if you take a career break (as many women have to do when they have children). With personal pensions, the holder pays a percentage of their salary into the fund (currently up to 17.5 per cent if you are under 35 years of age) and, when the pension matures (i.e. comes to an end – usually at retirement age), you get 25 per cent of the total as a lump sum, and the remainder buys an 'annuity' or yearly sum. Although many people still have personal pensions, the stakeholder plan is seen as better value.

TIP BOX

You may think retirement and the need for a pension are so far away you don't even need to consider them yet, but remember: the soone. you take out a pension the more it will grow. The difference between taking out a pension at 20 and at 30 is phenomenal.

ISAs

Also pretty new on the scene are **ISAs** (Individual Savings Accounts). They came into being in 1999 to replace the PEP (Personal Equity Plans) and Tessa (Tax-exempt Savings Account) plans, which were then closed to new investors. There are three main ways of investing in ISAs:

THE CASH ISA

If you are over 16, you can invest up to £3,000 cash a year into a cash ISA, which tends to offer slightly higher rates of interest than usual. All the interest the ISA earns is tax free.

Stocks and shares

If you are over 18, you can also invest in stocks and shares that are recognised on the stock market, including individual shares, gilts, unit trusts and bonds.

Life insurance

Again, if you are over 18, you can invest in life insurance, which is really intended for saving rather than for insurance purposes. Only a small amount of companies offer this ISA option.

THE MINI ISA

You can take out up to three mini ISAs in a year, and they can all be with different ISA providers if you so wish. You could invest £3,000 in stocks and shares with one provider, £3,000 in cash with another, and £1,000 in life insurance with yet another.

THE MAXI ISA

The limit you can invest in one year in a maxi ISA is £7,000 and is made up of £3,000 cash, £1,000 life insurance, and the remainder in stocks and shares. You can also invest the whole £7,000 in stocks and shares if you choose to do so. A maxi ISA can only be taken out with one provider. If you take out a maxi ISA, you cannot open a mini ISA in the same year.

All ISAs should be seen as medium to long-term investments of at least five years.

(Information on ISAs courtesy of Alliance and Leicester.)

So, now you know how you can save and in what format, it's time to take action and start saving for a rainy day. None of us know what the future will bring, but knowing you have made contingency plans will at least give you more control of your financial future.

HOW DOES YOUR MONEY GROW?

If you have never got into the habit of saving money then you probably know savings can quickly build up, but don't really have a clue as to what that means in concrete terms. Take a look at the chart below. This will immediately show you how your money grows, even if you save as little as £5 a week.

PER WEEK	ONE YEAR	TWO YEARS	5 YEARS
£5	£260	£520	£1,300
£10	£520	£1,040	£2,600
£20	£1,040	£2,080	£5,200

With £260, you could go on a budget holiday to Europe, and with £1,300, you could buy yourself an HP Wireless Network laptop, PDA and all in one scanner/printer/copier (and still have some change).

However, the way to make your money work best for you is to put it into some kind of savings plan where you earn *interest*. For every pound you save, you are given a percentage in interest, so if the percentage rate is 2 per cent for each pound saved, you would get an additional two pence. The interest rate can go down as well as up, and it is well worth looking around for the accounts that offer the most interest. Below is a chart of how much your money can grow depending on the interest rate (tax has not been taken into account in this chart). A lump sum of £1,000 has been deposited into a savings account and then 12 monthly deposits of £50 made each year. The total figure shows what the account would be worth after ten years, depending on what the level of interest is. (If the money had just been put aside without accruing interest, you would have saved £7,000.)

INTEREST RATE TOTAL AFTER 10 YEARS ON £7,000

2 %	£7,857
3 %	£8,336
4 %	£8,853
5 %	£9,411

The difference between just putting the money aside and putting the money into an account earning 5% interest is £2,411. Even the difference between an account earning 2% interest and one earning 5%, can mean an extra £1,554 in your pocket. However, there may be drawbacks to putting your money into a high interest savings account (HISA) – you may have to give a certain amount of notice before you can withdraw money from it (usually 30 days), and you may also have to keep the amount of money in the account up to a certain level to qualify for the higher interest.

Figure 5.1 Making your money work for you

CHAPTER SIX:

MONEY'S TOO TIGHT TO MENTION
How to avoid getting into debt

'I think you should never get in to debt as it is one of the worst things to do.'

James Bradley, 14

There are enough things in life to get stressed out about without having the worry of debt hanging over your head. However, it is a fact of modern life that most of us will owe money at some time. In fact, 95 per cent of students in higher education finish their courses in debt. You get into debt when you owe money to other people and don't have the resources to pay it back. However, some debts, known as **secured debts**, are planned (taking out a student loan or a car loan or getting a mortgage), while others, known as **unsecured debts**, are more accidentally accrued (running up a massive bill on your store or credit card). The trick is to know what you can afford to borrow and to pay back, and thus stay in control of the amount you owe, rather than letting it spiral hopelessly out of control. Far too many people who get into financial difficulties resort to 'ostrich with head in the sand' mode – basically, it gets too much for them to deal with, so they don't open statements or letters from the bank and don't come up with a strategy to sort it out, so the debt – especially the interest on the debt – quickly mounts up.

By this stage in the book, you should have a pretty good idea about balancing the money you have coming in with the money you have going out, and before we talk about the positive things you can do if your debt is beginning to run (and ruin) your life, let's explore the different ways people get into debt in the first place.

How people get into debt

1 14-year-old Jon really needs to top up his mobile phone but he's already spent his monthly allowance, so he asks his dad for a cash advance. His dad agrees to this on the condition the money comes straight out of Jon's next allowance. Jon is now in debt to his dad.

2 Nikki has just passed her driving test and wants to buy herself a second-hand car. She has enough for the deposit on the car but takes out a two-yearly loan from her bank to pay off the balance of the cost. As long as Nikki continues to make regular monthly payments, she has her debt under control. However, if she starts to miss payments, she could lose the car.

3 Rachel has spent a lot of money on her credit card because she has been travelling around Europe. What with flights, living costs and spending money on going out, she has now reached her upper borrowing limit, and she is shocked to see how much the monthly repayment with interest is going to cost her. She knows there is not enough in her current account to cover even the first repayment and, though she has a small, agreed overdraft, her credit card payment will take her over this – meaning she will incur further charges. So now she'll owe money to her bank as well as her credit card company, and Rachel is beginning to realise she may have a debt problem she doesn't know how to fix.

These three scenarios show the difference between a small debt that can be offset against future monies coming in (as long as Jon's dad doesn't let him make a habit of getting an advance!), a secured debt that has been planned and budgeted for (Nikki's car loan), and a debt that is only going to keep increasing until it is dealt with. It's a sad fact of financial transactions that the more you owe, the more the debt costs you in terms of interest payments – many credit cards also charge a penalty fee if you fail to meet the minimum monthly payment.

As mentioned before, as a nation we are now £1 trillion in personal debt, that is the equivalent of £17,000 for every man, woman and child in the UK. Mortgages and personal loans do make up a large proportion of this, but we owe a whopping £54 billion in unsecured debt, including credit cards. For those whose debts are not planned and not managed, debt can be a mental nightmare, even driving some people to despair and thoughts of suicide. However, there is now plenty of help available and the sooner you take advantage of it the better.

Where to get help with debt

■ For a start you need to talk to someone: keeping your troubles to yourself only serves to magnify them as they go round and round your head. Talk to your mum or dad, a good friend or a brother or sister: they may help you get a sense of proportion on the problem. If you can't talk to your family, then call ChildLine, a counselling service open to anyone up to the age of 18. You can talk to them in full confidentiality on 0800 1111 (see 'Resources').

▨ You can also talk to your bank or to your credit card company. If it subscribes to the Banking Code, part of its remit is to consider 'financial difficulty sympathetically and positively'. It makes sense for them to work out a repayment agreement rather than make you bankrupt. Contact them as soon as you see a problem occurring – the longer you leave it, the more it is going to cost you.

▨ Work out a plan for paying off your debts, putting necessities first. You may also consider switching the balance of your credit card to one that has a lower interest rate (see the 'Rate Tart' box at the end of Chapter 3).

PRIORITISING YOUR DEBT

1. First you need to work out how much money is coming in each month from part-time job, allowance, personal sources, and benefits.

2. Next, work out how much money is going out, putting the most important things, such as mortgage and rent, gas, electricity, transport and food, first. Remember to add in any regular credit payments that are paid monthly and then add in things such as telephone, clothes, etc.

3. See whether or not you have any money left over: if you have, you can use it to pay off your debts.

4. If you have several debts, list them in order of importance (such as being behind with your rent, your gas or electricity bills) because these are the ones you want to pay off first. Then you should deal with the debts on which you are paying the most interest (i.e. credit cards/store cards).

5. Once you have realistically worked out what you can afford to pay back each month, you must write to each of your

creditors asking if you can negotiate repayment of your debt. If they seem unhelpful, be persistent, or ask to be put in contact with somebody more senior.

6 Don't agree to pay back more than you can afford, you will just accrue more debt, and don't be persuaded to borrow from a loan shark, their interest is extortionate and they may turn nasty.

The best piece of advice anyone can give you is don't get into debt in the first place, especially if you know you are bad at budgeting. However, this is more easily said than done in a society where everybody seems to want to give you a loan or a credit card. Listen to what Dr Mark Hamilton, the presenter of BBC Radio 1's *Sunday Surgery* advice show says:

'Avoid the temptation to use credit cards unless it's absolutely necessary. If you do have to use one, pay it off as soon as you can and don't let it get out of control, which can happen all too easily.'

'I prefer to save up for the things I want, rather than wasting money on sweets and the first things I see.' **Adam Hicks, 14**

Ask for help from one of the following:

Advice UK

This was once known as the Federation Of Independent Advice Centres (FIAC), with a membership that includes local authority centres, charities and Information Shops for Young People. For your nearest centre, call 020 7407 4070 or visit www.fiac.org.uk.

National Association Of Citizens Advice Bureaux

This is the largest provider of free advice on debt and finances in general in the UK. For your nearest office, look in the phone book or ring 020 7833 2181 (in Scotland, 0131 667 0156) or visit www.nacab.org.uk.

National Debtline

This free, national telephone helpline gives expert advice over the telephone and can send callers a self-help information pack all about debt, free of charge. All advice is confidential and independent. The helpline is on 0808 808 4000 or visit www.nationaldebtline.co.uk.

For agencies in Northern Ireland, contact the **Association Of Independent Advice Centres** on 028 9064 5919 or visit www.aiac.net.

CHAPTER SEVEN:

THE FUTURE'S BRIGHT
Making money work for you in the long term

By now you should know a considerable amount about money and what it means to you. However idealistic and ethically minded you are, you will not be able to function in the modern world without coming into contact with 'filthy lucre' on a daily basis (even if you live in a commune where you barter for things/services, someone still has to pay the water bill and the council tax!). However, by having a positive, balanced approach to money and really knowing its worth, you can make it work for you rather than be at its mercy.

TIP BOX

Respect money, yes, fear it, no. Like anything else in life, once you become used to dealing with money in a responsible way, you'll wonder why you ever felt apprehensive about financial transactions in the first place.

Remember:

■ Think carefully before buying items – are you buying them through necessity or because some other emotional impulse (greed/envy/ depression/anxiety) is compelling you to? If it is something else, then address that issue and keep your cash in your pocket.

■ Think long term. It's all very well blowing your pocket money on the new Darkness CD the day your mum gives you the money, but what happens at the end of the week when you want to go to the new *Spiderman* blockbuster with your mates? The same goes for when you are in your first job – buying a second-hand banger might seem like a great idea, but what about paying for the road tax, the MOT, new tyres and repairs when it starts to fail in the future?

■ Be positive. Think of all the great things you can do if you learn to budget wisely and save your money.

■ Keep a sense of perspective. Nearly everyone (unless they happen to have inherited millions) will accrue some form of debt in their lives, but it doesn't mean the end of the world is nigh. As long as you are aware of what you are doing and in control of the debt, and not vice versa, it should not become a cause for concern.

■ Have fun! There are basically two types of spending – the type we have to do to survive (paying the rent, buying staples like toilet paper and food), and the type we do for pleasure (money we spend on entertainment, on luxury items, on treating ourselves). If you have saved hard for something special, then the pleasure is increased by your sense of achievement and pride that you did it for yourself and by yourself. You've earned it – now go and enjoy it!

'There is no point in being rich if you are not happy as well!' **Laura Wilson, 14**

Are you entitled to more money?

Here's something else to think about that will cheer you up – you may be entitled to money from sources other than those you have earned yourself or been given by your family. The government has recently introduced the Education Maintenance Allowance (EMA) of up to £30 a week, payable to 16-year-olds and to some 17-year-olds around the country. To be eligible, you have to be on a vocational or academic course for more than 12 hours a week and living in a household where the income is under £30,000 a year. To find out if you qualify for EMA go to: www.entitledto.co.uk or www.dfes.gov.uk, or request an information pack from 0808 101 6219.

If you are going to university and your parents' combined income is less than £20,480, your local education authority (LEA) will pay all your fees (apparently 50 per cent of students get the whole sum of their fees paid for them). Thus, you will be saving £1,150 – the maximum students are currently being asked to contribute to their fees, although this is set to rise in 2006. If your parents earn up to £30,501, you will have to pay a percentage of the tuition fees but not the whole sum. You may also be eligible for a student loan assessed by your LEA (or the Students Awards Agency in Scotland). The LEA tells the government-owned Student Loans Company (SLC) the amount the loan should be, and they send the cheque straight to your university (which is why you really have to have a bank account). You start repaying the loan in the April of the year after you graduate, but only if you are earning more than £10,000 per annum. From April 2005, you will start repaying your loan only when your income reaches £15,000. Nine per cent of your earnings are deducted directly from your pay cheque each month.

If you are going on to further or higher education, you may also be eligible for a scholarship, sponsorship or help with paying for your education via a charity. This will really depend on what course or degree you are taking. It will also depend on which college or university you are going to attend. The first thing to do is to contact the college or university directly and ask what scholarships are available. Also check if your local library has a copy of *The Directory Of Grant Making Trusts*, published by Charities Aid Foundation. You can obtain a copy from CAF, Kingshill, West Malling, Kent ME19 4TA. Trotman also publishes *University Scholarships and Awards* by Brian Heap that lists scholarships available to students from universities and other organisations.

They say 'it's the early bird that catches the worm', so you should explore all the sources of income that may be available to you as soon as possible.

Hopefully, now you have got this far through the book, you will have learned enough to face your financial future positively, rather than with dread. The following list of 'Dos and Don'ts' is just a reminder of what you have learned so far:

▓ Do keep a running balance of your financial transactions.
▓ Do devise a budget for your weekly or monthly spending.
▓ Do make sure you are getting all sources of income you are eligible for.
▓ Do get yourself a job, be it babysitting, a newspaper round, working part time or full time in the holidays.
▓ Do get into the habit of saving regularly.
▓ Do pay your bills on time (it saves you money in the long run).
▓ Do talk to someone as soon as you get into any difficulties.
▓ *Don't* get a credit card or store card unless it is absolutely

necessary, and then aim to pay the bill off each month so as not to accrue interest.

■ *Don't* ignore letters from your bank or bank statements.

■ *Don't* try to keep up with the Joneses if you don't have the necessary funds.

■ *Don't* borrow money from friends if you can possibly help it (friends are an even more precious resource than money).

■ *Don't* believe you are all alone if you get into difficulties: there are many people out there who can help you. Read all about them in the following 'Resources' section.

Your financial future can be a bright and positive one – just remember to be safe, be secure and be financially solvent!

'While I think love and friendship are important in having a happy life, I also think that without money it would be a great deal more difficult to be happy.'

Alice-Lara Waterman, 16

BANKS AND BUILDING SOCIETIES

Many, but not all, financial institutions subscribe to the Banking Code. This sets minimum standards of good service for banks, building societies and other providers of banking services. You can download a copy of the Banking Code from the British Bankers' Association: www.bba.org.uk.

Abbey

Under 'Personal Banking' on the website you will find an Account Chooser that will help you find the right account for your circumstances.

Tel: 0845 934 4900
Website: www.abbey.com

Alliance and Leicester

Alliance and Leicester has a FirstSave Account for young savers under 16 years old. You can open an account with £1 and, from the age of seven onwards, you can make your own deposits and withdrawals. The account gives a good rate of interest. It also has a Young Worker Current Account aimed at those between the ages of 16 and 18 who are in work, about to start work, or who need an account specifically geared for them. As long as you pay £100 per month into your account, you get free magazines and a linked savings account giving a higher rate of interest. If you are 18 or over, and paying at least £500 per month into the account, you become eligible for a Young Worker Credit Card.

Website: www.alliance-leicester.co.uk

Barclays

Barclays has a special under-18s account.

Barclaycard tel: 01604 230 230
Website: www.barclays.co.uk

Egg

Website: www.egg.com

Halifax

Tel: 08457 394 959
Emergency tel: 08457 203 099
Website: www.halifax.co.uk

HSBC

There are two HSBC accounts for young people. Livecash is aimed at 11- to 15-year-olds, and is very much an introduction to banking. It offers a high rate of interest (equivalent to a savings account rate) and comes with a Livecash card for withdrawals from ATMs, a paying in book, quarterly statements and interest on any credit balances. You can open the account with as little as £1, and each new account holder receives a mini clip radio.

The Right Track account is for 16- to 17-year-olds and is split into two – Right Track into Study is for those who plan to stay on in education, while Right Track into Work is for those who plan to start their careers immediately. Both services offer a Solo Debit Card (which can be upgraded to a Switch card if £300 is credited to the account per month), Internet banking, Direct Debits, the option to link to a savings account and a free BSM driving lesson at 17 with discounts off further lessons.

Tel: 0800 130 130
Textphone: 0800 028 0126
Emergency tel: 08456 007 010
Website: www.hsbc.co.uk

Legal & General

Legal & General do a UK index-tracking ISA that tracks the FTSE all-share index that includes over 650 top UK companies. Although these shares can go down as well as up, they tend to be quite healthy, and the beauty of this scheme is that there are no initial or withdrawal fees to pay, and you can start up the ISA with a minimum lump sum of £500 or an investment of £50 a month.

Tel: 0800 092 0092
Website: www.legalandgeneral.com/uk

Lloyds TSB

If you are between 11 and 18 years of age, you are eligible for a Lloyds' Under 19s Account. With this you can go to the Post Office to pay money into your account or, if you are over 16, you can bank by phone or Internet. There are no transaction charges. If you are under 16, you get a Cashpoint Card, and if you are 16 or over, you get an Electron Card which you can use both to withdraw cash and as a debit card. Interest is paid on any money in your account.

Tel: 0800 096 9779
Website: www.lloydstsb.com

NatWest

NatWest offers both special Student and Graduate Accounts.

Tel: 0870 600 0459
Website: www.natwest.co.uk

Royal Bank of Scotland

Royal Bank of Scotland has a variety of different accounts geared towards younger people. There are two savings accounts, as well as Route 15 (a current account for 11- to 15-year-olds), plus R21 (for those from 16 to 21 years old at college or university or in employment). The RBS group runs the Face 2 Face With Finance initiative – an in-school capability programme working with teachers to provide pupils with stimulating activities aimed to help them learn about money. If you would like to know more about Face 2 Face With Finance, contact your local branch of RBS direct. Check to see what it's all about on its website: www.rbsf2f.com.

Tel: 0870 600 0459
Website: www.rbs.co.uk

THE BEST ETHICAL BANKS

If you are concerned about the kind of businesses your bank invests in, and would like a bank that is more ethically aware as far as the

environment and society is concerned, there are several options open
to you. One way to go is to open an account with a building society.
As they are prohibited from lending money to companies irrespective
of whether or not they have a good ethical track record, they can only
fund mortgages. Otherwise, the banks below have all made an asset
out of their ethical policies.

The Co-operative Bank

The Co-operative has recently launched the Bonus Account for young
savers. The account is in conjunction with the conservation charity, The
Born Free Foundation. On opening the account, young savers receive
educational gifts made from recycled materials and an annual bonus
of up to £10 (if you are between 13 and 18 years of age). As the
amount saved increases, so does the annual rate of interest in the
account.

Tel: 08457 212 212
Website: www.co-operativebank.co.uk

Ecology Building Society

Tel: 0845 674 5566
Website: www.ecology.co.uk

Smile

Tel: 0870 843 2265
Website: www.smile.co.uk

Triodos Bank

Tel: 0500 008 720
Website: www.triodos.co.uk

ADVICE ON DEBT

Advice UK

This was once known as the Federation of Independent Advice Centres (FIAC), and has a membership that includes local authority centres, charities and Information Shops for Young People. For your nearest centre, call 020 7407 4070.

ChildLine

ChildLine is the UK's free, 24-hour helpline for children and young people. Trained volunteer counsellors comfort, advise and protect children and young people. If you really need to talk to someone about money issues and don't feel you can go to family or friends, then ChildLine can offer counselling and advice. This free service is available to anyone up to the age of 18 and is entirely confidential.

Freephone tel: 0800 1111
Website: www.childline.org.uk

National Association of Citizens Advice Bureaux

This is the largest provider of free advice on debt and finances in general in the UK. For your nearest office, look in the phone book.

Tel: 020 7833 2181 (in Scotland, 0131 667 0156)
Website: www.nacab.org.uk

National Debtline

This free, national telephone helpline gives expert advice over the telephone and can send callers a self-help information pack all about debt free of charge. All advice is confidential and independent.

Helpline: 0808 808 4000
Website: www.nationaldebtline.co.uk

Youth Access

Throughout England and Wales, Youth Access has a network of centres where young people can get advice and counselling. Call for your nearest Youth Access recognised centre.

Tel: 020 8772 9900
For agencies in Northern Ireland, contact the Association of Independent Advice Centres on 028 9064 5919 or at www.aiac.net

USEFUL WEBSITES

Connexions

Connexions is aimed primarily at 13- to 19-year-olds and gives excellent information on all aspects of their lives – from career choices to monetary queries.

Website: www.connexions-direct.com

Department for Education and Skills (DfES)

If you would like more information on Career Development Loans or on other aspects of funding higher education courses or vocational courses, the DfES has a special pack available.

Packs available from 0800 585505.
Website: www.dfes.gov.uk

Financial Services Authority (FSA)

This website is basically for consumers and will help you if you have queries or complaints about financial products or services.

Website: www.fsa.gov.uk

Guardian Unlimited Money

Whatever your query about finances and money, this excellent site will probably have the answer. To compare how the major banks stack up as far as account features, such as interest rates and charges, are concerned go to www.guardian.co.uk/money/compareandbuy and for advice on saving try www.guardian.co.uk/money/cashclinic.

Website: www.guardian.co.uk/money

Inland Revenue

When you first go into employment, you may be confused about which tax bracket you are in, and how your tax has been worked out. This website contains information on both tax bands and National Insurance, and you can order information leaflets directly from the site.

Website: www.inlandrevenue.gov.uk

National Youth Agency

This agency has an extremely informative site with a whole section on money, including how to manage it, what to do if you get into debt, and who to contact if you are experiencing financial difficulties.

Website: www.youthinformation.com

Office of Fair Trading (OFT)

The OFT has a website giving advice to consumers about all aspects of buying and paying for products, and it also has a consumer helpline. You can also obtain a leaflet entitled *Are You Store Card Smart?* from www.oft.gov.uk or from 0870 6060321.

Helpline: 08457 22 44 99
Website: www.tradingstandards.gov.uk

Short Change

Set up in conjunction with the CBBC series, *Short Change*, you can post your financial worries and queries on the site and get an answer from one of the presenters. It also contains consumer information.

Website: www.bbc.co.uk/cbbc/yourlife/shortchange

Support for Learning

If you are a student looking for funding, then this site is for you. It explains all the different subsidies, grants and tax breaks available to people going into further or higher education.

Website: www.support4learning.org.uk/money

This is Money

This great website (Consumer Website Of The Year) from the *Daily Mail* has information and advice on everything from pensions to personal loans, as well as all the latest news from the financial world. Compare and contrast loans here.

Website: www.thisismoney.co.uk

USEFUL BOOKS

Do take a look at the other books in Trotman's *Real Life Issues* series, which offers practical advice, tips and hints on overcoming problems that many teenagers face.

Real Life Issues: Addictions, by Stephen Briggs
Real Life Issues: Bullying, by Emma Caprez
Real Life Issues: Confidence and Self-Esteem, by Nicki Household
Real Life Issues: Coping with Life, by Jonathan Bradley
Real Life Issues: Eating Disorders, by Heather Warner
Real Life Issues: Sex and Relationships, by Adele Cherreson
Real Life Issues: Stress, by Rozina Breen

Directory of Grant Making Trusts
The Charities Aid Foundation publishes a booklet that lists all the places you can go to find funding from charitable sources for further education and higher education courses. If your local library does not have a copy, contact CAF direct.

Address: CAF, Kingshill, West Malling, Kent ME19 4TA

University Scholarships and Awards by Brian Heap
Published by Trotman, this book lists scholarships available to students from universities and other bodies.

Students' Money Matters by Gwenda Thomas
Published by Trotman, this book provides essential budgeting information and tips for anyone preparing to go into higher education.